Dear Teacher,
You are special to me because . . .

you are a
good
storyteller.

[name] Rocco Fanelli
[date] 6/24/06

Dear Teacher

I Will Always Remember You Were My Teacher

sigmund brouwer

(and friends)

Nashville, Tennessee

Project Editor: Kathy Baker

Design: Lookout Design Group, Minneapolis, Minnesota

ISBN 1 4041 0055 5

Printed and bound in the United States of America

www.thomasnelson.com
www.jcountryman.com

www.coolreading.com

COMMANDED TO TEACH

Teach them the right way to live
and what they should do.

—EXODUS 18:20

THE HEART OF A TEACHER

Let the teaching of Christ live
in you richly. Use all wisdom to teach
and instruct each other . . .

—COLOSSIANS 3:16

INTRODUCTION

As an author, it has been my privilege to travel to hundreds of schools in the United States and Canada, and I have learned a new respect for teachers.

My former perspective of what teachers did was based on my years as a student. And students, of course, see very little of the prep work, marking, counseling, coaching, and dealings with parents and administration that take up so much of a teacher's time and energy. It was easy for me to believe the myth that teachers "only work from 9-to-3."

As an adult re-entering the school world, however, I realized that teachers often devote ten or twelve hours a day—plus weekends—to their jobs.

Then I discovered how stressful it is to actually teach. Few of us consider how physically difficult it is to maintain discipline in a room of twenty-five to thirty energy-filled children, let alone to direct that energy into learning.

Our memories mislead us further, because we recall classrooms filled with relatively similar groups of students. As recently as twenty years ago, a single-parent child was a rarity. Now, sometimes more than half of the children in a class carry emotional or developmental scars from missing one or even both parents. Previously, teachers could plan lessons for a group generally at the same learning level; now, a fifth grade teacher, for example, will face students who range in ability from second to seventh grade, yet be expected to teach them all equally.

Teachers are called on to do much more than simply teach. Under difficult conditions, these men and women also teach basic living skills, and often are the only positive role models some children see.

This was reflected in the overwhelming response from students when I asked for letters for the *Dear Teacher* project. Almost without fail, thousands of students described their own teachers as the best. Each letter showed that teachers were making a difference.

That's why I was glad for the chance to work on this book. Too often, teachers don't hear how much they are loved. And needed.

Here are what the students have to say. And I hope that *Dear Teacher* is a way for all of us to say Thank You!

Sigmund
(and friends)

THINGS WE HAVEN'T
LEARNED YET IN SCHOOL,
BUT WANT TO ASK:

Dear Teacher

could you tell me . . .

. . . how old you are because you say you're
100 years old and I don't believe it.
I would also like to know how diamonds
are made.

Morgan, age 9

. . . would I be a good teacher and why is
math so confusing?

Alyssa, age 11

. . . why do you need an answer book?

Victoria, age 11

. . . why should you get mad at me for
something I didn't do?

Dara, age 10

p.s. I didn't do my homework

. . . why do you get paid for being around
us nice kids?

Shannon, age 10

. . . why Jesus hasn't come yet?

Josef, age 10

. . . why God says that parents should have complete control over their children?

Reed, age 10

TEACHING IS A GIFT FROM GOD

The LORD has given . . .
the ability to teach others.

—EXODUS 35:24

A TEACHER'S PROMISE

I will instruct you and teach you
in the way you should go;
I will guide you with My eye.

—PSALM 32:8, NKJV

. . . why do we have health class? I don't
know why we have to learn about sex.
Sarah, age 10

. . . what do worms drink and do they?
Kristen, age 9

. . . why have history if it was a long time ago?
Henton, age 11

. . . who were the presidents? Why were they
better choices than the other people
who ran? Did they promise more stuff?
Jillian, age 10

. . . why aren't I growing?

Daniel, age 12

. . . what is a loontic and where does one live?

Anel, age 10

. . . why do we have so many words?

Mackenzie, age 8 1/2

. . . what does it look like
in the staff room?

Mady, age 8

. . . how come you get to
sit in the staff room
and eat cake while we
have to stay outside
when it is freezing?

Shannon, age 10

THINGS WE LEARNED
ALL BY OURSELVES IN SCHOOL:

Dear Teacher

here's advice for
other students...

. . . don't tell the teacher how to do his job.

Jessica, age 10

. . . if your teacher asks you how you got into grade 5, don't reply, "Good question."

Eamon, age 10

. . . never cheat, because if the teacher doesn't see it, God will.

Haily, age 10

. . . have the funnest time of your life in school because when you're old it won't be fun.

Jenna, age 10

. . . don't stick clay up your nose.

Ryan, age 9

. . . don't throw garbage at Jordan.

Jordan, age 11 1/2

. . . never accidentally mark your place in a
library book with gum.

Alyssa, age 11

THINGS WE LEARNED
FROM YOU THAT AREN'T PART
OF THE CURRICULUM:

Dear Teacher

the single best thing you
taught me about life is...

. . . the teacher is always right.

Donovan, age 11

. . . how to be a good roll model.

Betty Elizabeth, age 9

. . . if you're ever teaching kindergarten, always remember to bring ear plugs and a loud speaker.

Aneta, age 9

. . . never waste life. If you're steaming over something, you should go on with your life, don't waste it on that little thing. There will be bigger and more worse things to steam over later.

Chelsea, age 11

. . . the only thing to fear is fear itself. And also bullies.

Victor, age 11

. . . God created us as who we are and there
is nothing we can do to change that.

Sami, age 10

. . . life is nothing without Jesus.

Taylor, age 10

. . . that I am an outstanding person.

Ryan, age 11

. . . to listen more than I talk.

Adam, age 13

. . . everyone is different in different ways,
and everyone is equal.

Jessica, age 10

. . . the thing you taught me about life is
that it is not the worst thing.
Austin, age 10

. . . the grass is greener at other schools.
Brianna, age 12

. . . don't give your cat spiked egg-nog.
Jessica, age 12

WHY ARE YOU SO SPECIAL:

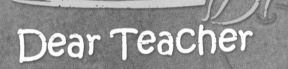

Dear Teacher

what I will always remember
about you is...

. . . you eat chocolate like a car needs gas and oil.

Jeremy, age 9

. . . how you always end up with chalk dust on your back.

Samantha, age 11

. . . the smile we saw so rarely.

Penny, age 10

. . . that you were always soft but firm.

Ashley, age 11

. . . that you really like that scripture
board in the classroom.

Candace, age 12

. . . that you were the nicest teacher I
had. So far.

Brady, age 8

. . . that you teached me.

Mickie, age 8

. . . the way you teach, not like every teacher does. You do it from your heart.

Sincerely, Alyssa, age 10

. . . the way you stare into my eyes for so long without blinking and then out of nowhere you say, "SEE ME AFTER SCHOOL" for no reason.

Jay, age 13

. . . when I look back in my memory, you
will always be there when I need you.
Brian, age 12

. . . how you always showed kindness to
me, no matter how grouchy you are.
Nicole, age 11

. . . that you retired at the end of the year.
Phillip, age 12

. . . Horse feathers, my child!!! I will always
remember that you say all these
strange expressions I'd never heard
until you became my teacher.

Kelsea, age 10

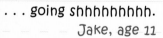

. . . when you are reading, you
give good expression.

Brogan, age 10

. . . going shhhhhhhhh.

Jake, age 11

WHAT WE LEARNED ABOUT
HOW YOU TEACH:

Dear Teacher

if I had one piece of advice to pass
on to your students next year ...

. . . never plant a flower in her shoe for a
class project.

> Greg, age 12

. . . don't ruin passing notes for the rest of the
class by passing them at the wrong time.

> Amanda, age 11

. . . say her kids are cute and she will love
you forever.

> Scarlett, age 11

. . . if you are in trouble, make her laugh.

> Zachary, age 11

. . . be careful, she loves to trick you and
give you homework.

Jennifer, age 12

. . . never do anything behind her back.
She can see everything.

Brandon, age 10

. . . always go with what the teacher says.
(And never groan.)

Julian, age 10

. . . try not to be afraid of fifth grade. It's
not as hard as you might think.

Violet, age 10

Dear Teacher Here's Advice for Your Students Next Year...

. . . don't make him mad. When he gets
   mad, he can YELL! (don't burst out
   laughing or he'll get even more mad.)

Amanda, age 12

. . . be nice and try not to make her cry.
   (She cries easily.)

David, age 12

. . . bring ear plugs because your teacher
   sings really bad.

Marica, age 10

. . . bring mints so that when she has
   onions you will be prepared.

Jenay, age 13

WHAT WE WILL NEVER FORGET
DURING OUR YEAR WITH YOU

Dear Teacher

do you remember...

. . . the other day when people were saying why
they liked you so much? Some probably just
did it to get out of spelling.

Natasha, age 12

. . . when a student yelled MOUSE and
you screamed and jumped across the
classroom?

Nicola, age 11

p.s. there was no mouse

. . . when my friend put my frog in your shirt?

Julie Ann, age 8

. . . when the speaker was on and you were
in the washroom and we could hear?
Sean, age 10

. . . when you heard something crunching on
your clothes and saw your hamster had
eaten a extra large hole in your skirt?
Megan, age 9

. . . when in religion class you said 'puberty'
and you meant to say 'poverty'?

Mary, age 10

. . . when you forgot my name? IN THE
MIDDLE OF THE SCHOOL YEAR.

Alyssa, age 10

WHAT WE LEARNED ABOUT
BOYS AND GIRLS:

Dear Teacher

the advice I would give
about love is...

. . . that it's DISKUSTING.

Joseph, age 10

. . . I don't get love and I don't know how to get it.

Tiphanie, age 9

. . . it's stranger and stranger, but eventually you will get it.

Jeremy, age 9

. . . it's the most wonderful thing in the world, but sometimes it hurts. When you're in love, it feels like the greatest thing ever, but sometimes the one you love will run from you. It feels like someone tied a hook around your insides and dragged it five miles. So if you're going to fall in love, you better be ready for a five-mile trip.

Pauline, age 12

. . . if you have it, you'll make it through
the day.

Anna, age 10

. . . love is a privilege, not a right, and you
should not take love for granted.
Because some countries don't have
that privilege.

Christina, age 11

. . . it can be used for you. And against you.

Janya, age 12

. . . it is not for kids.

Tanisha, age 11

. . . leave it until grade seven.

Courtney, age 12

. . . to not rush it, wait, but don't wait too long.

Kenna, age 10

. . . don't date until you're married.

Lauren, age 9

. . . it is good if you want to have kids.

Sheila, age 8

. . . it's not all about kissing.

Robert, age 9

. . . never watch kissing on television.

Edward, age 8

. . . ewwwwwwwwwwww!

Kyle, age 7

. . . love one another and tell them a Bible verse.

Dominique, age 8

. . . to have someone love you is a gift, but to love them back is a treasure.

Sian, age 12

. . . never have a chile or bean burrito for lunch and then sit by your crush.

Bridie, age 10

. . . never bug your love about her hair.

Daniel, age 8

. . . everything has its beauty, but not
everyone sees it.

Aazan, age 12

. . . it's easier to love someone than hate them.

Claire, age 9

. . . never ask what if questions.

Stephanie, age 8

ABOUT SPIRITUAL MATTERS:

Dear Teacher

if you and God had a chance to talk,
I think it should be about...

. . . giving boys more grace.

Mark, age 10

. . . how smart girls are in your class.

Emily, age 11

. . . us. And about how good we are.
(Except at lunch time.)

Melissa, age 10

. . . where He came from.

Lindsay, age 10

. . . the questions that no one can answer.
Like how did He create people?

Keneth, age 10

. . . why God made humans and not aliens.

Gabriel, age 11

. . . how if you get sick, it's not a big deal, but if God gets sick we're really going to be messed up.

Joe, age 12

. . . whether I'm going to heaven or not. And by the way, if you don't mind, put in a good word for me.

Sarah, age 11

. . . how does God listen to a lot of prayers at the same time?

Kristy, age 11 (close to 12)

Dear Teacher

if I had a chance to talk to God
about you I would tell Him. . .

. . . how funny you are and kind because when people don't put in a capital, you don't yell.

Jesse, age 10

. . . how nice you are and how you are always thinking of being a movie star.

Adeline, age 10

. . . that you are the second sweetest woman in the world.

Shyang, age 9

. . . that you were the greatest teacher
     I ever had in my life.

                    Nataliah, age 8

. . . you are the best teacher in the world.
     And to help you stay like that.

                    Chrystal, age 10

. . . that you are the best and you're
     kind and you deserve to live for
     1,000 years.

                    Bridget, age 9

. . . how good you teach us in Religion.

Angelica, age 9

. . . how much you love Him.

Nicholas, age 10

. . . how hard you tried to love everyone
including the trouble makers.

Nicole, age 11

HOW WE'D LIKE
TO HELP YOU IN THE WAY
YOU HELPED US:

Dear Teacher

the most important advice
I would give you about life is. . .

. . . chocolate isn't a food group.

Corbin, age 9

. . . never catch a hamster in a vacuum.

Dean, age 11

. . . if you're still teaching in a couple of years, watch out because my brother will be here soon.

Jeremy, age 10